Exploring Dilemmas in Anti-Racist and Anti-Discriminatory Practice with Young Black Street Robbery Offenders: The Experiences and Viewpoints of Social Workers in a London Youth Offending Team

Monograph

ISBN No. 1

Contents

Glossary of Terms

I have used a number of abbreviations throughout this monograph. In the forthcoming literature, I will firstly use the full terminology and then I will use the abbreviations. The abbreviations are as follows:

ADP	Anti-Discriminatory Practice
AOP	Anti-Oppressive Practice
ARP	Anti-Racist Practice
BSRO	Black Street Robbery Offender
CBT	Cognitive Behavioural Therapy
CDA 1998	Crime and Disorder Act 1998
DTO	Detention and Training Order
PC	Person Centred
PSR	Pre-Sentence Report
TC	Task Centred
WSRO	White Street Robbery Offender
YJB	Youth Justice Board
YOT/s	Youth Offending Team/s

Introduction

1.0 Introduction

1.1 Setting the Scene

On 15th August 1972, an offence was committed that was to have an unprecedented effect on British society for many years to come. This day an elderly widower, by the name of Arthur Hills, was robbed and stabbed to death near Waterloo station as he was returning home from a theatre **(Haralombos, 1995)**. This tragic incident was by no means a "new" crime in itself – violent street crimes had been committed as far back as the nineteenth century by "garrotters" – but the media coverage suggested otherwise. Indeed, this case was the first time that a specific crime in Britain had ever been labelled as a "mugging" in the press. The front page headline of the 17 August 1972 edition of the Daily Mirror, for example, was an encapsulation of the real threat that journalists believed that this crime posed to society: "As Crimes of Violence Escalate, a Word Common In the United States Enters the British Headlines: Mugging. To our Police, it's a frightening new strain of crime" **(cited in Hall et al, 1978: 3)**.

Between September 1972 and August 1973, a further sixty events were dramatically focussed on by the media and reported as "muggings" **(Haralombos, 1995)**. Just three months after the killing of Mr Hills, for instance, Robert Keenan was attacked by three youths in Birmingham. His assailants knocked him to the ground after robbing him and returned to the scene two hours later, where he still lay, and further assaulted him. The media frenzy continued and judges, politicians and the police joined them in stressing intense concern over the seriousness of this crime. Some commentators, such as **Hall et al (1978)** argue that a "moral panic" was created where there was an extremely strong reaction and widespread fear of this phenomenon.

Three decades later, the moral panic about "mugging" (which has been replaced by the more politically correct terminology of "street robbery" in recent times) has not gone away. Newspaper coverage of the offence is still as ferocious and prevalent as ever with related daily stories dominating the press – "Blind Woman Mugged for £10" **(Daily Mirror, February 26 2003: 2)**; "Woman Stabbed in Street Robbery" **(Sunday Mirror, December 15, 2002: 16)**; "Street Crime Worsening, Says Poll" **(Coventry Evening Telegraph, September 18, 2002: 10)**; "Man Stabbed in Face in Mugging Horror: Man, 26, Beaten by Gang of Four" **(Coventry Evening Telegraph, February 25, 2003: 1)** - and a recent poll showed that street robbery is generally the most feared crime in Britain today[1] **(Independent, November 21, 2002: 10)**.

Similarly, although time has moved on three decades since the moral panic over street robbery began, it has been suggested that the generally held assumption that a specific group is responsible for the majority of these offences has remained the same. Indeed, the media-frenzied imagery of the 1970's which first named street crime, but particularly "mugging", and correlated it to the actions of black (predominately male) Afro-Caribbean youth is still potently evident in today's press: "70% of Muggers are Black in Robbery Hotspots" **(The Times, January 10 2003: 11)**; "Nearly 15, 000 stabbings, robberies and even murders…most linked to 300 yards where £1m of crack-cocaine is dealt each month. Is this the most dangerous street in Britain? Investigation: The Standard spends 24 hours in the London borough where the police fight their biggest battle against crime" **(Evening Standard, January 30, 2003: 16)**; "82% of London Underground Victims Identify Muggers As Being Black" **(The Sun, January 10, 2003: 11)**; "Blacks Over-represented in Prison Statistics" **(The Sun, April 1, 2003: 7)** and "Stop and search of Black People up by a Third in London" **(Evening Standard, Nov 7, 2002: 4)**. Furthermore, it has been argued that the conceptual attribution of street robbery to black people has been internalised by society **(Gilroy, 1987)** and a number of writers have depicted the notion that these views, towards black people have not simply manifested in

[1] This claim is based on a poll carried out by the Independent newspaper which surveyed diverse groups – males and females, people of different races and ages – and concluded that, overall, more people fear being victims of street robbery than any other crime.

people's minds on an individual basis, but have developed on a far deeper and complex level:

> "That these views are prevalent in popular culture, the media coverage of 'hard news' and political commentaries is sufficient evidence of the breadth and depth of racism in Britain, but it is their institutionalisation as all-pervasive which transforms imagery into ideology" **(Scraton and Chadwick, 1996: 290).**

The concept of "institutionalised racism" has become more notorious in the last few years. This notion lay dormant for nearly two decades after **Scarman (1981)** denied its existence in the police or other state agencies. However, after the damning **MacPherson (1999)** report on the Stephen Lawrence murder enquiry greater validity was given to the assertions that had long been made by commentators who had analysed the methods that the criminal justice process has treated the black people with which it deals – that the methods were representative of ferocity, inequality and racism:

> "It is clear that in terms of access, recruitment, training and development the criminal justice institutions and their professions have failed to deal with their well-established traditions of discrimination. Further, it is clear that racism is endemic in the policies, priorities and practices of the criminal justice institutions" **(Scraton and Chadwick, 1996: 292).**

Studies into racist practices within the court and prison systems and also within the police and probation services have been well-documented, but very little research has been carried out to date with regards to Youth Offending Teams (YOTs). This is probably due to the fact that YOTs are a relatively new institution. Indeed, the Audit Commission's **'Misspent Youth' Report (1996)**, which focussed on ways of curtailing the soaring rates of youth crime, suggested that this objective could best be achieved by the creation of an agency which could deal with all factors that placed young people at risk of offending. The Crime and Disorder Act 1998 (CDA 1998), which reflected the Labour Government's vow to drastically reduce youth crime, acted on these recommendations by setting up the multi-disciplinary agency of YOTs **(s37 CDA 1998)**. These multi-disciplinary teams (or multi-agencies) comprise social workers, probation officers, education, police and mental health workers and a number of voluntary agencies and are overseen by the Youth Justice Board (YJB) for England and Wales. Through the service delivery of its YOTs, a central aim of the YJB is:

> "That all interventions are delivered fairly, consistently and without improper discrimination, in a way that values and respects the cultural and racial diversity of the whole community **(National Standards, 2002: 4).**

1.2 Objectives of Study

This monograph seeks to investigate whether the anti-discriminatory approach is being successful in YOTs by examining the experiences and viewpoints of eight social workers who are supervising the extremely marginalised group that is black street robbery offenders (BSROs). The aim of the dissertation is to explore the dilemmas that may surface in social work practice with this clientele and the ways in which social workers feel that they can be ameliorated. I have developed five main themes to investigate. These are: -

- The use of Anti-racist practice (ARP) and/or Anti-discriminatory practice (ADP) by social workers – How do these value systems underpin social work practice with BSROs and how successfully are they being implemented?

- The use of ARP and/or ADP by other YOT social workers – How do these value systems underpin other YOT social workers' practice with BSROs and how successfully are they being implemented?

- Transferring social work theory into practice – How effective are the three main social work models used in work with young offenders – person-centred (PC), task centred (TC) and cognitive behavioural therapy (CBT) - and therefore with BSROs?

- Efficacy of the multi-disciplinary team – How successful has the multi-disciplinary YOT been in work with BSROs and in the implementation of ARP and/or ADP?

- Implications – What are the implications of these themes on social work practice with BSROs?

Indeed, the overall aim of this project is to conduct a study that signifies a movement towards "evidence based" social work practice. This approach derives from the debate of whether social policy owes more to art or social science **(Dean et al, 2000)**. The New Labour Government has argued that it is a quasi-science government, that is moving towards a pragmatic "best practice" approach to policy making **(Dean et al, 2000)**. Blair has claimed that evidence-based policy making and implementation **"means learning from mistakes, seeing what works best…."**. This study aims to achieve a similar approach where dilemmas in current practices with one of the most marginalised groups in society can be identified and explored and suggestions for future (more effective and efficacious) social work practice can be made.

The remainder of this introduction will define the key terms that are used throughout this research and explore the characteristics of the London borough that is the focal point of this study. **Chapter one** will evaluate the value systems that are recommended in anti-racist, anti-oppressive and anti-discriminatory practice; review a selection of literature and research around effective usage of the PC, TC and CBT approaches; critically review literature that assesses the efficacy of multi-disciplinary teams and briefly explore the pro-social approach. **Chapter two** will outline the research methods that I elected to use for this study and will analyse their suitability and the data collection process. Ethical issues will also be incorporated into this section. I will present and evaluate my findings within the five aforementioned themes in **Chapter three**, before concluding the findings from my study in the final chapter.

A central position in this monograph is the focus on ADP. However, I did not want to limit myself purely to issues of race, because my findings have also led me to focus on the areas of young women, dyslexia and learning difficulties (within the ADP area of black race).

1.3 Definitions

Black Street Robbery Offenders (BSROs)

BSROs in this dissertation refers to young people who:

- are deemed by the law to be responsible for their criminal actions (ages 10 – 17)
- who have been convicted of street robberies
- are of Afro-Caribbean, African, or Mixed Race (African/Caribbean/White) heritage

Chapter One

2.0 Literature Review

2.1 Racism and Anti-racist practice in social work

At the outset, it needs to be noted that very little literature exists to specifically address the issues that can arise between social workers and BSROs. However, there is much literature that focuses on racism and anti-racist practice (ARP) in social work and the probation service and a lot of this literature is directly applicable to social work practice with BSROs. This section therefore reviews some of the most well-known work, giving an overview of the values that need to be present, and avoided, in order to implement effective anti-racist social work. I will then offer a critique of anti-racist theory and practice by reviewing the broader approaches of AOP and ADP.

In her book "Anti-Racist Social Work", **Dominelli (1997)**, a self-proclaimed white practitioner, focuses on what she sees as an urgent need for a transformation in the field of social work, where stereotyping and the reinforcing of racist practices are abolished. Her book shows how significant the issue of racism is for the practice of (white) social work with black people. **Dominelli (1997)** suggests that if (white) social workers are not able to understand the ideology and dynamics of racism, they will fail to deliver effective services to black communities and will reinforce the inegalitarianism and inequality that is evident in society.

Dominelli (1997) suggests that racism consists of three main types that interact with each other – individual or personal racism, institutional racism and cultural racism. Individual racism, she suggests, is where attitudes or behaviours depict a negative viewpoint towards people from different racial groups. Institutionalised racism is argued to be where public power or authority is used to blame excluded groups for their lack of social prosperity and to keep them at the bottom of the social hierarchy. **Dominelli (1997)** portrays cultural racism as being encompassed by beliefs, values and ideas which are endorsed by the superiority of white culture. She argues that it is cultural racism which juxtaposes and reinforces both institutional and individual racism and therefore advocates its eradication in social work practice.

I have found that although **Dominelli's (1997)** work is extremely challenging, she does appear to contradict herself on occasions. For example, on one hand she argues that if white social workers begin to relate to black clients on the basis of equality, they will become better practitioners and that agency policies and practice will be improved. However, on the other hand, her critique of the 'colour-blind' and 'universality of treatment' approaches could still lead to practice where white social workers treat black people unfairly. **Dominelli (1997)** argues that "colour-blindness" (through the concept of 'universality of treatment') is a racist practice because it is based on the assumption that everybody is the same. She argues that this approach ignores structural inequalities, such as systemic racism. However, some would argue that in order to achieve anti-racism and equality, black people do need to be regarded as being the same as white people because this will be the stepping stone to equality of treatment and opportunity. **Dominelli's** critique of universalism could be therefore be viewed as an argument against equality for black people, rather than an argument in support of it.

A second critique I have of **Dominelli's** work is that she fails to acknowledge that it is not just white people who can be racist, or discriminatory, towards black people - people of other races can also harbour such prejudices, not least black people themselves (who may be from other cultures). In chapter three, my findings will demonstrate a case of a mixed race social worker (of Afro-Caribbean and white British descent) who challenged a black African social worker for displaying racism towards a black Afro-Caribbean client. Section **2.2** will provide further critiques of **Dominelli's** work.

Despite certain drawbacks in her work, **Dominelli's (1997)** book does offer some astute suggestions as to how ARP can be implemented in social work and her work is therefore applicable to my study. Indeed, she suggests that all social workers use their experience, sense of self and personalities in order to establish relationships with clients, but that (white) social workers need to question the assumptions that they may hold about black people. **Dominelli (1997)** argues that the engagement in this process is crucial to effective ARP. With regards to work with BSROs, this process is instrumental. When taking into consideration the facts that black offenders are amongst the most marginalised groups in society and that BSROs have committed a crime that is well-feared by the general public, the possibility that racism may surface in work with this group is not unlikely. Furthermore, the first value requirement of the General Social Care Council (the new governing and training body of social workers who took over from CCETSW in 2001), is that social workers: "identify and question their own values and prejudices and their implications for practice" and this is similar to the recommendation made by Dominelli (except that hers is specifically related to race) and myself in the conclusion to this monograph (except that my recommendation is related specifically to work with BSROs).

2.2 Critiques of ARP in social work – Anti-oppressive practice and Anti-discriminatory practice

In her article "Connecting Anti-racist and Anti-oppressive Theory and Practice: Retrenchment or Reappraisal?" **Williams (1999)** reviews some of the major critiques of anti-racist theory and practice in social work.

One argument against ARP that **Williams (1999)** assesses is with regards to the problematic nature of single issue positioning. She suggests that such single standpoints have the potential to create tension amongst oppressed groups where competition emerges as they fight separately to attain their goals, rather than in unity. Indeed, oppressed groups that are characterised by class, race, gender, age and sexuality may therefore become unproductive to the pursuit of equality.

Another argument reviewed by **Williams (1999)** is the assertion that categories such as 'black', 'black perspectives, 'race, and 'racism' not only lead to a reductionist aggregation of ethnic differences, but can also lead to confuse social work practice.

Indeed, it has been suggested that such conceptualisations can actually generate stereotypes in social work practice and exacerbate and perpetrate discriminatory attitudes. The implications of this for a client group such as BSROs could therefore be detrimental as this group is already marginalised.

Additionally, **Williams (1999)** highlights the fact that an array of the debates within anti-racist social work have been scrutinized for producing answers to complex social phenomena with oversimplified and formulaic responses. The presenting of certain ARP arguments as being representative of 'the way forward' in social work practice have been branded as pragmatically unworkable.

A further critique of ARP that was reviewed by **Williams (1999)** was that it curtails the experiences of black people by presenting it merely as a reaction to the domination of the white race. The tendency to portray black people as being victims and to depict their lives as being difficult has been dominant in a lot of ARP social work literature. The implication of this could be that many black clients are disempowered and that self-fulfilling prophecies can emerge or exacerbate. This could have serious consequences for work within YOTs with a group like BSROs where the empowerment of the client is seen as being essential to successful preventative work **(Fitzgerald et al, 2003)**.

Williams (1999) suggests that the paradigm for the future of the perspectives in social work that focus on oppressed groups is anti-oppressive theory and practice. She argues that this approach would represent all oppressed groups and enable social workers to help them overcome their difficulties.

It would appear that **Williams (1999)** has presented the major critiques of ARP in a clear and coherent manner. Reviewing her work has certainly made me aware of the limitations of the approach and led me to a major criticism of my own. Indeed, the ARP approach has such a specific focus that it could lead to the neglect of other significant attributes. Using BSROs as an example, since the ARP approach could limit the social worker to focussing on the (black) race of the offender and the problems that that being black may have caused, there are other structural factors that could potentially be ignored. For instance, my project has led me to discover that some BSROs face issues such as learning difficulties, dyslexia and sexism (where the offender is female). ARP may therefore be too narrow an approach to identify such issues. These issues will be reflected on in detail in chapter three.

A weakness in William's own work however is that she appears to be advocating the use of AOP in social work on the grounds that it will benefit all oppressed groups. This would be beneficial to a client group such as BSROs, who are argued to be oppressed by an array of writers, but not all groups would actually be classed as being 'oppressed'. Offenders who are white, male and middle-class, for instance, are unlikely to be viewed as 'oppressed', but rightly have as much right to social work intervention as offenders who may be deemed to be 'oppressed'.

Taking the drawbacks of ARP and AOP into consideration, it has been suggested that an approach that is totally universal and integrated may be more effective – an approach that excludes nobody and nothing and tackles oppression head on. **Thompson (1997)** argues that this approach is ADP. He suggests that social work practice will only be totally effective at tackling inequality if a form of equality-seeking practice exists as a unitary whole, as opposed to surfacing as anti-sexism plus anti-racism plus anti-ageism and so on. **Thompson (1997: 33)** advocates ADP as the way forward because it seeks to eradicate all forms of discrimination and oppression:

> "An approach to social work practice which seeks to reduce, undermine or eliminate discrimination and oppression, specifically in terms of challenging sexism, racism, ageism and disablism and other forms of discrimination or oppression encountered in social work".

With specific regard to BSROs, it could therefore be argued that ADP could capture all of the forms of injustice experienced by this group and seek to eradicate them.

2.3 Racist practices in social work with black offenders

Denney (1992) takes on a perspective similar to **Dominelli (1997)** in his book "Racism and Anti-Racism in Probation". However, he focuses on a more specific client group and social work area by examining the social construction of black pathology within the probation service. Indeed, **Denney (1992)** uses ethnographic material to illustrate ways in which racism within this institution affects the social work service that is delivered to black offenders and offers suggestions as to how this can be ameliorated.

One of the most damning examples **Denney (1992)** uses in his work to stress the racist practices in probation work is with regards to his findings on the recommendations made in social-enquiry reports (now called PSRs in YOTs and probation). He discovered that a number of significant qualitative differences were discernible in reports written for black offenders in comparison to white offenders. He provided evidence that concluded that probation officers were far more likely to use 'conventional' forms of explanations in their reports on white offending, which would distance the offender from the offending behaviour. **Denney (1992)** suggested that this was often combined with a tendency to use explanations that were dominated by excusing or victimising terms in their reports, which would ultimately lead to a non-custodial recommendation to the sentencer. In comparison, although there was no significant difference between the number of non-custodial recommendations made for white and black offenders in the research, **Denney (1992)** pointed to the inclusion of derogatory terms in the reports of black offenders that were not present in those of their white counterparts. He concluded that the featuring of negative connotations and statements made it more likely that sentencers would be harsher when sentencing black offenders.

These findings by **Denny (1992)** are important to my study because the same practices may be found in YOTs. Many YOTs do have a 'gatekeeping' system where all reports are checked for discriminatory comments, but discrimination does not have to be overt. Covertly racist comments may not be identified by the 'gatekeeper'. Indeed, given that the numbers of black prisoners has doubled in England and Wales from since 1997 and that black inmates are still receiving longer sentences than white people for the same crimes **(Home Office, 2002 and The Voice, Monday April 7, 2003: 2)** it could be suggested that this problem is not just due to racism from the courts and the police, but could also be due to information presented in PSRs to the courts.

Another significant aspect of **Denny's** findings was related to the differences that occurred between probation officers' form of assessments, intervention and outcomes of interventions with black and white offenders.

Denny (1992) points to the work of two writers who both advocate taking the individual client as a starting point, **Whittaker** and **Sheldon**, to illustrate the apparent lack of consensus that exists in defining assessment. Indeed, he suggests that **Whittaker**, likens assessment to a social-treatment model:

> "A joint process through which the worker and client explore and assess physical, psychological, and social conditions as they impinge on the client and then attempt to relate their findings to the range of social problems experienced by the client in a manner that yields objectives for change as well as a plan for action" **(Whittaker, 1974: 159 cited in Denney, 1992: 95)**

Denny (1992) argues that although **Sheldon** writes from a perspective that leans more towards the behaviouralist school of thinking, his perception of assessment whilst still an individualistic approach is linked to evaluation from the beginning of all work with social-work clients:

> "Behavioural assessment is concerned with the identification of behaviours which would be useful and reasonable to perform. Such assessment also takes into account the consequences of actions for all concerned in a social situation" **(Sheldon, 1982 cited in Denney, 1992: 96)**.

Denney (1992) argues that these two views of assessment suggest that a diverse range of activities could be called social work assessment. He argues that since ambiguity is present in the work of just two writers, it is not surprising that probation officers, who also start from an individualist perspective, also have different viewpoints on the features that make up this social work task. What **Denney (1992)** suggests is unfortunately surprising, however, is that assessments, interventions and outcome are affected by the race of the offender. He discovered that the majority of probation officers interviewed defined success with regards to establishing a relationship with the client, or preventing offenders from receiving custodial sentences. **Denny's (1992)** study found that work with black offenders was less successful in each outcome, in that probation officers were less likely to be successful in diverting a black offender from custody and that they were likely to experience other difficulties in engaging with black offenders.

The task-centred (TC) model was an intervention that **Denney (1992: 114)** suggested was essential to changing "offender-behaviour patterns" of black and white offenders. This is because the task-centred model is based upon a clear mandate for action and focuses on client agreement. The overall aim is to move from problem to goal, creating tasks that will lead to ameliorative change for the client **(Milner and O'Byrne, 1998).** However, because of the problems that existed between some probation officers and black clients, the outcomes of interventions were not as successful as they could have been. This finding provides a powerful argument for the assertion that work with black offenders can be affected by social workers who harbour prejudices. This point was emphasised by **Fitzgerald et al (2003: 80)**:

> "The disproportionate involvement of young black people in street crime raised issues of ethnicity and offending for many workers – whether white or of minority ethnic origin. These again tended to be resolved individually, raising the possibility that in some Yots black young people would encounter differing attitudes towards their offending, depending on which worker they were allocated to".

Although **Denny's** findings did not include an analysis of their application, there is a strong possibility that the other two main social work models that are used in work with offenders – person centred (PC) and cognitive behavioural therapy (CBT) – could also result in reduced efficacy in work with black offenders because of discriminatory attitudes of social workers.

The PC approach lays a primary emphasis on the quality of the relationship between the worker and the client. It encourages the facilitation of a comfortable atmosphere in which therapy can take place and effective working relationships can be developed **(Mearns and Thorne, 1988** and **Rogers, 1951)**. There are three significant qualities which must exist in the attitude of the worker to accomplish success in a PC based intervention: genuineness (authority or congruence), where the therapist shows that they are a genuine person; unconditional positive regard, where the therapist shows that they genuinely care for clients in a non-judgemental manner and empathic understanding, where the therapist is able to enter the client's world in order to understand what is going on in their mind **(Gross, 2001)**. However, it can be argued that if social workers display discriminatory attitudes or hold prejudiced beliefs, the success of such an intervention with BSROs is likely to be limited.

The same can be said of CBT, where a strong relationship between the worker and the client is also instrumental to the attainment of a successful outcome. CBT is a dynamic model for helping people to change and acquire new skills. It aims to help the client identify their automatic thoughts, become aware of their emotions, link their thoughts to behaviour and change their automatic thoughts to more suitable ones **(Trower et al, 1988)**. Again, although **Denny (1992)** did not directly include CBT in his study, his findings provide a strong argument that racism in work with black offenders could also affect the effective application of CBT with them.

2.4 The multi-disciplinary YOT and encompassing problems

It is important to note that although social workers usually control the casework in YOTs, many of the offenders participate in work with other members of the YOT **(National Standards, 2002)**. As was outlined in chapter one, these other professionals include probation officers, education, police and mental health workers and a number of voluntary agencies and the overall aim of this is to identify and ameliorate risk factors in young offenders in order to prevent further offending **(National Standards 2002)**. These objectives will therefore be regarded by almost all citizens as being satisfactory, but the same consensus does not exist in society and amongst writers about the ways in which some of these groups of professionals interact with certain members of the community. Indeed, aside from some of the problems that have occurred between social workers and probation officers and the black community (some of which have already been highlighted in this Monograph), the police and the mental health field have also come under fierce attack for certain methods of practice with black people. For instance, the police have long been scrutinized for their overtly racist stop and search policy **(Fitzgerald, 2001, Fitzgerald et al, 2003, Roberts, 1982, Kinsey et al, 1986)** and the racist attitudes of many of its police officers **(Macpherson, 1999, Home Office 2000** and **Young, 1994)** to name a few factors. Within the mental health field, one example of a well-documented issue is the fact that there appears to be racist practices evident in forensic psychiatry, such as the unnecessary diagnosing of schizophrenia of many black people **(Fernando, Ndegwa** and **Wilson, 1998)**. These issues may have significant implications when certain members of these professions work with a client group such as BSROs, for two significant reasons. Firstly, some workers from these fields may hold racist attitudes and stereotypes which may ultimately affect the success of their interventions with BSROs. Secondly, BSROs may be wary of working with professionals who are labelled as being 'racist':

> "Young blacks are said to be suspicious of white-dominated welfare organisations and their suspicions are confirmed by the actual or alleged failure to help them " **(Cheetham, 1982: 75)**.

Additionally, it has been suggested that there are other problems that can emerge in multi-disciplinary teams. In "Delivering Multi-Agency Partnerships in Community Safety", **Crawford (1998)** suggests that achieving successful multi-agency partnerships is difficult and that the problems that surface within them are rarely acknowledged.

Crawford (1998) argues that there are two key structural dynamics that exist in partnerships. The first he puts forward is the existence of conflicts over ideology, purpose and interests, where deep structural conflicts emerge between the parties that work together in partnership. The second is the existence of differential power relations between the partners. He suggests that issues such as different access to resources (both human and material) and debates over expertise and power relations can cause a state of deterioration in the aforementioned conflicts. **Crawford (1998)** asserts that that the juxtaposition of these dynamics can lead to detrimental factors in the implementation of partnership work: conflict avoidance may surface as parties attempt to avoid conflict and this results in the neglecting of real issues that need to be addressed; a strategy of multiple aims may surface where a number of objectives are set for a project that are often broad and lacking in clarity and informal or hidden relations may surface as a result of conflict avoidance, where decisions may be taken outside of formal and public processes.

Crawford (1998: 220) argues that problems of accountability are regular occurrences in multi-disciplinary teams. He suggests that the complex nature of the institutions means that accountability is often obscured. Furthermore, he suggests that this can lead to problems in getting certain groups, particularly those who are over-represented and marginalised within the criminal justice system "on side". Indeed, these critiques put forward by **Crawford (1998)** suggest that the multi-agency approach could have a negative impact on the service delivery to groups such as BSROs.

2.5 The pro-social intervention model

So far, this chapter has predominately explored the issues that can affect an efficacious social work service to BSROs by focussing on the problems that can be evident in social work practice. However, I feel at this stage that it is also important to highlight the fact that BSROs can also affect the service that they receive and hinder social workers (or other workers in the YOT) in their interventions.

In "Working With Involuntary Clients", **Trotter (1999)** puts forward a model that is based on behaviouralist theory called the pro-social approach. The model proposes ways that workers can make the best use of their skills with involuntary clients and achieve maximum results in the process. **Trotter (1999)** suggests that the pro-social model is effective because it contains a number of principles that enable the worker and the client to work collaboratively in a problem-solving environment.

Indeed, **Trotter (1999)** argues that the findings of his study of corrections have indicated that there are four main aspects of the pro-social approach: the identifying of pro-social comments and actions, which involves the worker identifying and thinking about things they would like their clients to think and say; providing rewards or reinforcement for pro-social actions and comments, where for example a client is praised by the worker for positive behaviours or comments; modelling pro-social behaviours, where the worker models the behaviour that they want the client to aspire to and the challenging of undesirable behaviour, where the worker expresses disapproval of anti-social or undesirable comments or actions by the client. **Trotter (1999)** suggests that the pro-social model is successful because it enables the client to learn by encouragement as opposed to by discouragement.

Chapter Two

3.0 Research Methods

This section seeks to evaluate the research methods that were selected for my study in depth.

3.1 Focus of inquiry and gaining access

I have had an interest in issues related to BSROs for a number of years not least because I had touched upon the area when I took my Sociology A-Level and when I studied a Criminology unit as part of my Social Policy and Management degree. **Silverman (1993)** suggests that where a researcher's previous education has equipped them with several research ideas, a useful strategy that can help in the pursuit of a researchable problem is that of using sensitivities. This involves a researcher thinking about how previously learned knowledge can sensitize them to various researchable topics and issues. **Silverman (1993)** distinguishes four types of sensitivity: historical, where a researcher should assess the relevant historical evidence when setting up a topic to research; cultural sensitivity, where research is shaped by forms of cultural representation that may be influenced by 'experiences'; political, which shows the vested interests behind current media 'scares' and contextual where phenomena is not viewed as being uniform, but are recognised as taking on particular meanings in different local contexts and cultures depending on certain factors (such as who the audience is).

The first three sensitivities put forward by **Silverman (1993)** had a potent influence on my deciding upon my research area. I was historically sensitive to exploring dilemmas in social work practice with BSROs because I have long been aware of the marginalisation that this group have experienced in society. I was culturally sensitive because although I am not (and do not intend to ever be a street robber), I am a young black male and have experienced discrimination. I was politically sensitive because I have been aware of the way that BSROs have been depicted in the media for the last three decades (see introduction). However, I am aware of the potential bias that these sensitivities could cause in this monograph and have taken steps to reduce the risk of this. This will be discussed later in section 3.8, where I write about my interactions with the respondents.

Rubin and Babbie (1997: 19) state that "one of the chief goals of the scientist, social or other, is to explain why things are the way they are and social work practitioners routinely formulate tentative explanations as part of the problem-solving process that they apply to everyday practice dilemmas". I had received feedback from some BSROs, I had worked with at a YOT, about the 'hostile' treatment they had received and had also received information from other social workers I had contact with, with regards to this. I therefore decided that it would be challenging to explore some of these dilemmas with a view to contributing to a 'problem-solving process'. I therefore had a research focus, but I had to obtain access and formal permission from the manager of a YOT.

Bell (1999: 37) states that "no researcher can demand access to an institution or to materials". Bearing this in mind, I had to decide which YOT I wished to conduct my research at. I elected to base my dissertation on an inner London YOT. I therefore wrote letters to the managers of four YOTs, to maximise the likelihood of receiving a response at least one of them. I actually received responses from three of the managers, but elected to attend a meeting with only one of them because of time constraints. At the meeting, I explained to the YOT manager the objectives of my research and emphasised the fact that the organisation and the names of respondents would be anonymised. I was granted access to interviewing social workers, who were interested in participating, and secondary sources which had been produced by the agency.

A major reason why I was granted permission by the YOT manager was because they felt that the results of the research would be beneficial with regards to them knowing whether and how their staff is practising ARP, AOP and/or ADP. Indeed, **Bell (1999)** suggests that the negotiation stage should involve the reaching of a mutual decision with regards to access of the final report. As I was researching an extremely sensitive issue and was not certain what the outcome would be, I did not agree to provide a full copy of the report. In order to maintain confidentiality and protection of the respondents, I agreed to provide the YOT with a summary of the main findings. I then wrote to the workers that I wanted to include in my sample, inviting them to participate in my research.

Getting access to respondents for the quantitative part of my research was not as simple however. I wrote letters to the managers of seven YOTs explaining the objectives of my research and asked if they would distribute the questionnaires to their social workers. However, even when I telephoned the managers of these YOTs, I received a lukewarm response. These difficulties, combined with others, led me to abandon the quantitative side of my research.

Seeing that I had obtained consent from the agency and my research sample, the next task was to decide upon the methods of data collection I was going to use in my research.

3.2 – Research Options – Qualitative and Quantitative Methods

Qualitative data

Silverman (2000: 8) suggests that qualitative data "exemplify a common belief that they can provide a 'deeper' understanding of social phenomena". Indeed, because qualitative research studies produce phenomena in such detail, and from multiple perspectives and meanings, the subsequent data is extremely rich and descriptive **(Rubin and Babbie, 1997)**.

The main advantage of qualitative data is that because it provides such rich and detailed data, it is able to depict true accounts of people's way of life, experiences, attitudes, feelings and beliefs **(Patton, 1990)**. For this reason, qualitative data are viewed as being more valid than its quantitative counterparts. This is one of the reasons why there has been an increased tendency to use the qualitative method in social work research, particularly when the efficacy and effectiveness of practice is being assessed. **Abbot et al**

(1998: 170) suggest that "qualitative 'open' methods are more and more used in research into social policy and professional practice and are becoming increasingly acceptable to administrators and policy makers".

The qualitative method is not free of drawbacks however. One disadvantage is that qualitative methods are unreliable because of the subjectivity that is present during the data collection process **(Silverman, 2000)**. In other words, if the study was repeated, the chances of the same results being produced are unlikely.

Additionally, because qualitative data is often collected by methods such as interviews or participant observation, the presence of the researcher could affect the answers or behaviour of the respondent. This can occur in two ways. Firstly, the 'Hawthorn Effect' can have a detrimental impact on a study. This is where respondents or participants are aware that they are being studied and respond to this knowledge as a result **(Haralombos, 1995)**. Secondly, interviewer bias can affect the responses given by a respondent.

Moreover, there is the problem of 'anecdotalism' in qualitative data. As **Bryman (1988: 77)** argues:

> "There is a tendency towards an anecdotal approach to the use of data in relation to conclusions or explanations in qualitative research. Brief conversations, snippets from unstructured interviews...are used to provide evidence of a particular contention. There are grounds for disquiet in that the representativeness or generality of these fragments is rarely addressed".

Indeed, because of the qualitative researcher's ability to be selective by giving certain examples to explain a phenomenon, but neglecting other data in the process, the validity that has been attributed to qualitative data can be called into question.

Quantitative data

Quantitative data was described by **Fuller and Petch (1995: 200)** as being "data which is in numerical form, lending it to producing frequency counts, averages and percentages and which may be analysed by statistical methods". Quantitative data are likely to rely on one indicator, or a few indicators, which can be administered in a few minutes and which allow comparisons to be made **(Rubin and Babbie, 1997)**. A large number of people have to be used to test the hypothesis or hypotheses of quantitative research to ensure representativeness.

The main advantage of quantitative data is that the data it produces are regarded as being reliable. This means that if the study was to be repeated, the same results are likely to be produced **(Silverman, 2000)**. In addition, the quantitative method allows a large amount of respondents to be used and in an inexpensive and non time-consuming way. The results can also be analysed and placed into categories relatively easily.

As with the qualitative method, quantitative research and data has its disadvantages. **Silverman (2000)** identifies a number of these. Firstly, although quantitative data is argued by its researchers to be value-free, the pursuit of phenomena that is 'measurable' can mean that values can actually emerge in research. This is because ambiguous or problematic concepts are often taken on in the analysing of quantitative data. Secondly, the fact that quantitative research involves little or no contact with people or the actual 'field' can be a weakness. This is because many researchers (who are usually from the qualitative field) feel that it is important to establish some form of relationship with respondents. A third criticism is that a totally statistical approach can make the development of hypotheses from data highly problematic.

Additionally, because quantitative data is collected predominately by survey interviews or questionnaires, bias can emerge from the researcher who has designed these tools. Indeed, questions may be phrased in ways that lead respondents into giving certain answers **(Fuller and Petch, 1995)**.

3.3 Methods selected

I originally wanted to find out about the social work service that was delivered to BSROs from the client group themselves. I felt that this would provide me with a better picture of the type of practices that social workers and other workers within YOTs use in their work and enable me to evaluate them. However, it became apparent that qualitative data collection with BSROs as the respondents was not feasible for ethical and practical reasons. Indeed, obtaining permission from the young people, their parents and young offenders institutions (for those BSROs who had received DTOs) would have been highly problematic.

I therefore decided that my study could be implemented using social workers as the respondents. This method allowed me to obtain information from social workers about their own social work practice (i.e. on an individual basis) and about the practices of other workers (organisational level). Indeed, considering that my research is focussing on issues that are highly sensitive and controversial, I did not want the respondents to feel intimidated or threatened. I therefore felt that it was important that my research also focussed on the respondents' perceptions of ARP and ADP on an organisational level (i.e. within the YOT) and did not personalise matters by focussing purely on the social workers' individual practices.

I also took on board the fact that my research was sensitive, controversial and potentially personalising to the respondent when deciding upon my choice of method. I felt that it was important to gain detailed and in-depth responses from the respondents because my study is seeking to assess efficacy and effectiveness of social work practice and aims to represent a best practice and evidence-based approach. Indeed, I hope to conclude my monograph by suggesting ways that interventions with BSROs can be improved in the future. Therefore, I did not feel that this could be achieved solely by the quantitative method. However, because of the juxtaposition of the facts that I am black and that my research is sensitive, I was aware that this may cause some respondents to be dishonest if a qualitative method was used. **Haralombos (1995: 842)** suggests that "consciously or unconsciously, respondents might give the sort of answers they believe that the interviewer wants to hear rather than saying what they truly believe". Therefore, I decided that the quantitative method could overcome this problem because anonymised postal questionnaires could produce more honest answers from respondents.

I therefore decided to use triangulation in my research. **Rubin and Babbie (1997: 365)** argue that "by combining qualitative methods with survey research methods, we can benefit from the strengths of survey research while we offset its weaknesses regarding superficiality, missing social context, inflexibility, artificiality, and questionable validity". I hoped that using both methods would result in a study which effectively incorporated the strengths of both approaches and would subsequently diminish the disadvantages associated with using them separately.

However, the aim of triangulation did not go according to plan. Time constraints meant that it would not have been possible for me to design, conduct and analyse the qualitative interviews and to design, send out and analyse the quantitative questionnaires. Therefore, after discussion with my research methods tutor, it was decided that the quantitative side of my research had to be left out. This could have negative implications on the results of my data and thus on my findings.

Before I decided to collect the data in my study by using semi-structured interviews, it was important to evaluate the types of interviews that were available to me to determine which was more suitable for my study. The three types available were structured interviews, unstructured interviews and semi-structured interviews.

Abbot et al (1998) suggest that structured interviews consist of a pre-scheduled and pre-coded checklist which is filled in by the researcher in response to the respondents' answers. One advantageous aspect of this type of interview is the fact that direct comparisons can be made between responses because each respondent will be asked identical questions. In addition, structured interviews have a fairly simple structure, through the pre-coded checklist, which means that a large number of respondents can be interviewed. However, it can be argued that structured interviews give researchers too much power, in that they give them the scope to decide upon the issues which will be included and left out of the checklist. It is because of this reason that I decided against using the structured interview in my study. I wanted the respondents to be able to give me detailed responses and did not want to restrict them in their answers.

Bell (1999) suggests that as they have no structured format, unstructured interviews allow respondents to give extremely detailed, lengthy and in-depth answers to a research area. Advantages of this type of interview is that it can produce information that may allow the researcher to view the subject matter from a variety of perspectives and that it can provide a wide breadth of information. However, I decided not to use unstructured interviews because in my opinion the disadvantages outweighed the benefits. Indeed, a lot of time is usually needed to analyse information gathered from structured interviews and I had an extremely tight schedule. Also, I did not feel that I was an experienced enough researcher to deal with the large amounts of information I would likely have received had I used this method.

Bell (1999) suggests that semi-structured interviews are the intermediate method of data collection in that they lie in-between structured interviews and unstructured interviews. Semi-structured interviews usually have pre-identified themes and issues contained in them, but because of their open-ended nature respondents are not restricted or led into answering a question in a specific way. A key advantage is that semi-structured interviews allow researchers to obtain detailed, concise and in-depth information about specific areas, but allow the quantity of the information to be controlled (i.e. they allow answers to be given that are not too long and that are not too short). Additionally, the time that analysis of semi-structured interviews requires is manageable. Bearing in mind these advantageous factors, I decided that this method of data collection was the most suitable for my study.

3.4 Research Sample

When sampling is analysed by researchers, a lot of attention is paid to the representativeness, reliability and validity of the cases. However, **Silverman (2000: 102)** suggests that with regards to qualitative research, it is often the scenario that a case would have been chosen because it "allows access". Indeed, this was applicable to my research sample where it could be suggested that the type of sampling technique I used was snowballing. **Haralomobos (1995)** argues that snowballing is a specialised type of sampling that is only used when other methods are not feasible. Snowballing involves using personal contacts to build up a sample of the group to be studied. At the earlier stage of my research, I explained the objectives of my study to a worker at the YOT I was based at for my second year placement. This worker is very prominent in the youth justice field and has worked in it for many years. This worker gave me the names and contact details of four YOT managers who she knew very well and although I had to write introductory letters to them all, three of them had already been made aware of my study and myself by the worker when I contacted them. This snowballing technique enabled me to interview eight social workers at the YOT.

3.5 Ethical Issues

Rubin and Babbie (1997) suggest that there are four main ethical issues that must be addressed by social work researchers – voluntary participation and informed consent, potential harm to participants, anonymity and confidentiality and analysis and reporting.

Rubin and Babbie (1997: 60) argue that "all participants must be aware that they are participating in a study, must be informed of all the consequences of the study, and must consent to participate in it". I took this ethical consideration very carefully. Indeed, after I had been granted permission to conduct my study by the YOT manager, I wrote to the social workers that I wanted to interview. I heard back from eight of the ten and had telephone conversations with them all. During these conversations I explained the objectives of my study and obtained their consent for participation. These two points were reiterated at the beginning of the actual interviews.

The key reason why I did not offer to give any of the respondents a copy of the full report (see section 3.1), was to make sure that the participants would not be harmed in any way and to ensure anonymity and confidentiality. With regards to the former, I have also ensured that no names of respondents are used in the report.

With regards to analysis and reporting, I agreed to give a summary of my main findings to each respondent, whether they are negative or positive. Indeed, **Rubin and Babbie (1997: 63)** argue that "there is an unfortunate myth that only positive discoveries are worth reporting".

3.6 Gathering the data

The data collection process for my study involved the implementation of semi-structured interviews with eight social workers from the Community Supervision Team of a YOT. These respondents were initially contacted by letter late in 2002. I contacted them again in February 2003 to arrange mutually convenient interview dates and times.

It had been recommended by my research, pathway and personal tutors to devise an interview schedule. I used my five research themes (as outlined in the introduction) to develop the schedule. In order to test the schedule, I conducted a pilot study with an experienced social worker from my practice placement. Although this pilot was helpful in helping me prepare for the actual interviews, I found that my schedule appeared to cover the themes in detail and therefore required minimal amendments. Indeed, I only had to re-phrase and add in a few additional questions (see appendix).

The actual interviews took place between February 10th 2003 and March 28th 2003. The duration of the interviews were between an hour and one and a half hours and were conducted in the respective YOT building in rooms that were private. All of the interviews were tape recorded, with the permission of the respondents.

3.7 Analysing the Data

The interviews I conducted were transcribed in their entirety, as I felt that reading the transcriptions would be the most effective way of identifying themes. I based the identification of themes on the work of **Glaser and Strauss (1967)** that used the term grounded theory to describe a process of discovering theory from data. They argued that theories that were empirically generated from (and grounded in) observations of the world were more valid than other theories. I was able to identify themes from my data by placing data into specific categories and these themes are explained in detail in chapter three.

3.8 Strengths and Limitations

A major strength of the research that I conducted was that although I had to abandon the quantitative aspect of my study, I feel that the method that I did use allowed me to obtain some very important information about the use of ARP and ADP in social work with BSROs. As will be illustrated in chapter three, I received feedback that could not only ameliorate social work practice with BSROs, but other groups as well. In addition, I am pleased with the way that I conducted the qualitative interviews with regards to being non-directive and making the respondents feel comfortable with me. **Haralombos (1995: 840)** argues that being non-directive means "to refrain from offering opinions, to avoid expressions of approval and disapproval". I feel that it is important for all researchers to practice this technique, but it was especially important to my study because of the sensitivity of the area/s.

A major limitation of my research was related to the fact that I had to abandon the quantitative aspect of it. I feel that anoymised questionnaires would have allowed me to have obtained a better understanding of social worker's perceptions of BSROs because respondents may have been totally honest (since I would not have been present and would not have known who they are). I am not claiming that the respondents were dishonest in the qualitative interviews I carried out, but there is a possibility that some could have been considering my research area and the fact that I am black.

<u>Chapter Four</u>

4.0 Findings and Discussions

In this chapter, I will be focussing on themes that emerged from the qualitative interviews that I conducted with the social workers. I will be presenting examples of quotes that represent these themes to back up my discussion and have organised them under headings.

It is important to stress that this chapter is of a descriptive nature. It was not possible given the word limit and time allocated to this project to analyse my findings using a more complex form of analysis such as content or discourse analysis. Therefore, after I have given a descriptive presentation of my findings, I have summarised and analysed the implications of these findings for social work practice and related them back to the literature review that formed chapter one.

A lot of the themes that emerged from my interviews did confirm the existence of dilemmas in social work practice with BSROs. However, there were some themes that also disproved this existence. I will now present these negative and positive findings from my research using the themes that were identified in the introduction.

4.1 The use of ARP and/or ADP by the interviewed social workers

4.1a Positive findings – disproving of dilemmas

ARP as an essential tool

Most of the social workers were aware of the ARP perspective and stressed that they felt that it was an important tool in work with BSROs. They argued that it helped them to focus on the injustice and inequality that black people face and helps in social work intervention. Indeed, ARP was described as a guide to good practice with BSROs where the success of interventions depended on the ability of the social worker to recognise the difficulties that the offenders face (and have faced in the past) because of their race:

"You have to be aware of the fact that these young people............. are black. It's an important issue to them. Most of them have experienced a lot of racism and if you don't recognise that in your work with them then it'll be hard to establish strong relationships with them"

"When you are working with a group like BSROs, you can't ignore the fact that they are black. I don't know what it's like to be black and to be discriminated against in that way. I have to use an approach that helps me understand them"

"So many of these kids have been.....treated like rubbish because they are black. You know, by the police and the courts. These kids need you to acknowledge that they are black and that they have experienced racism. ARP is fundamental to my work".

All of the social workers claimed that they were not prejudiced towards black people and that they did not hold stereotypical views. They emphasised, however, that the ARP approach prevents such thoughts from entering their minds because it governs their work with all ethnic minority clients, such as BSROs on both a personal and institutional level. These findings could suggest that the ideas of anti-racist writers such as **Dominelli (1997)** have had an influence on the work of the social workers at this YOT. **Dominelli (1997)** placed a lot of emphasis on the role of (white) social workers in eradicating personal, cultural and institutional racism in social work. It appears that the respondents share a similar viewpoint, in that they believe that by placing the race of the BSRO centre-point, they are moving closer to the attainment of these goals.

ARP as a means of acknowledging power differentials

The social workers suggested that their use of ARP was a way of them acknowledging the power that they have over BSROs. However, it was emphasised that the existence of this power was not just from a social worker/offender perspective, but also from that of a white/black approach. They argued that the mutual acknowledgement of this by the worker and the client is important because it helps BSROs to be aware that they will not be discriminated against and helps to develop and strengthen the working relationship:

"Certainly most of the black offenders I have worked with are suspicious of me because I am a white person in a position of authority. After they have been treated unfairly by other similar people or agencies.....it is not surprising. I always acknowledge the issue of power in my sessions and make sure that they are comfortable. If they are not, we can discuss the issue further. That is why ARP is important. It helps tackle difficulties like that".

"The issue of power is so....powerful that you have to address it. If you don't, it will remain in the back of their minds and yours and will cause friction".

Indeed, the social workers believed that ARP enabled them to acknowledge power differences and cited this as a key factor to successful social work interventions. This belief by the respondents again reinforces an argument purported by **Dominelli (1997)**, where she suggested that the ability of social workers to recognise power differences was essential to the empowerment of the client (with regards to enabling them to better themselves), the social worker (with regards to enabling them to make successful interventions and successfully implement ARP) and ultimately to fighting racism. This will be discussed further shortly.

ADP as an essential tool

All of the social workers emphasised the fact that ADP underpins their work with all clients, but particularly with stigmatised groups like BSROs. They argued that ADP is essential in working with such groups because it involves recognising the oppression that they face and helps in the pursuit of good practice:

"My God ADP is such an important part of my work. I mean how could I claim to be a good social worker if I didn't practice it? You couldn't be a very efficient practitioner, with regards to working with a group like BSROs if you don't practice ADP".

"ADP is instrumental in work with all clients, but is particularly crucial when I am working with a group like BSROs. That group is so marginalised and oppressed that it would be impossible to implement effective preventative work without ADP. ADP guides me in my work. I'm not prejudiced anyway, but even the most unprejudiced person could say or do something which could be interpreted by the client as being discriminatory. I would not risk that. My client's perceptions of me mean a lot to me".

"To me, ADP is the most important aspect of social work. Without it you're screwed".

ADP as a means of identifying and focussing on wider structural issues

Whereas many of the social workers stressed the significance of ARP in work with BSROs, it became evident that they were also aware of its limitations. The social workers informed me of the fact that most of their BSROs have issues and problems that a focus on ARP would not encompass. They suggested that ADP is so important because it enables them to identify factors that may contribute to the long-term offending behaviour of BSROs:

"I feel that you can see the wider picture with ADP. Well of the six BSROs that I have as clients at the moment, four of them have learning difficulties. It....upsets me in a way you know because these young people have been failed by the education system. Black kids are ten times more likely to be excluded than a white kid for the same misdemeanour. It's so unfair. It's............hardly surprising then that young black people are overrepresented in street robbery statistics. If they get expelled from school and other schools won't take them on, the street is the next place for them to loiter".

"No disrespect to ARP, but everything's not just about race. I had a BSRO as a client who was difficult to engage with. He would try and communicate, but he would sometimes be incoherent. His previous social worker got....well annoyed and the case was reallocated to me. I knew that something was holding him back. After I made a referral to xxxx my suspicions were confirmed –he was dyslexic and had learning difficulties. You can identify more issues when you look at things from a wider angle".

"She received a two year DTO for that, when males committing the same offence get a year. It wasn't just because she was black, but also because she was female. The courts are harsher on females. When you are black and female they're really tough. Her mother wants to appeal because she fears that xxx will become a hardened criminal when she gets out".

Here, the answers from the respondents supports the work of **Thompson (1997)**, and to a lesser extent that of **Williams (1999)**, where it was suggested that social work practice that focuses on a specific strand, or on a few specific groups, runs the risk of being exclusive. Indeed, the use of a more universal approach like ADP by the respondents enabled factors such as learning difficulties, dyslexia and sexism to be identified and interventions devised to overcome these, thus tackling risk factors that could have potentially led to long-term offending by the BSROs.

4.1b Negative findings – Confirmation of dilemmas

Negative comments about black youth

Although, none of the social workers confessed to holding racist or discriminatory views towards BSROs or black people, I did find it concerning that there were a number of stereotypical, generalising and sweeping statements that were made by some of them when discussing their practice of ARP and ADP with BSROs. I did not realise all of these at the time of the actual interviews, but when I was listening to and transcribing them some became clear:

"A lot of BSROs have had problems at school. They might generally be more disruptive, but that is no excuse for treating them unfairly. I couldn't discriminate like that. ADP symbolises good social work practice. ".

"You can't get upset by the attitude problem that they (BSROs) have. It's nothing personal. I think a lot of black offenders feel threatened by white practitioners. That's why ARP and ADP are so important".

"Black youngsters don't really have any positive role models. I mean.....Mike Tyson and gangster rappers are not good role models for young people of that age".

"Street robbery is becoming a culture amongst black youth. Yes there is poverty, deprivation....but I think that looking cool is important to them too"

"ADP is very important. It helps to overcome....issues. For example, I had a black client who had robbed a pregnant woman. I found it difficult to work with him because of that. He was poor, but I couldn't have done that if I had been penniless. ADP reinforces your commitment to fair practice".

"When you find out who the offender has robbed.... It's usually shocking. You think 'that could've been my daughter'. But you can't let it affect your work".

I did not take any of these comments, by some of the social workers, as being intentionally racist, nor do I claim that any of the workers who made these comments are. However, they do raise issues about how some social workers perceive groups such as BSROs and this could have important implications on their practice with them. Indeed, the aforementioned comments support the research of **Denney (1992)** who highlighted the stereotypical comments that some probation officers made about black offenders and raised concerns about the effectiveness of the social work that these workers would implement with black offenders.

4.2 Respondent's views on the use of ARP and/or ADP by other social workers in their YOT

4.2a Positive findings – Disproving of dilemmas

ARP and ADP as effective tools

The social workers from the YOT informed me that their fellow social work colleagues believe that ARP and ADP are important and representative of "good practice" with all clients, but particularly with regards to oppressed groups such as BSROs. There appears to be a general consensus that these two approaches are crucial to effective preventative work:

"All of the other social workers on my team believe that ARP and ADP are important"

"They all know that if they want successful outcomes with a group like BSROs, then ADP is a must. There's no doubt about it. They know that you can't discriminate against an offender and expect them to respond positively to interventions".

This could suggest that the theories of practice that have been recommended by writers such as **Dominelli (1997)** and **Thompson (1997)** appear to have been internalised and transferred into practice by the respondents. In addition, it could be suggested that the respondents' values are in line with the objective of the YJB that was quoted in chapter one (page 11).

4.2b Negative findings – confirmation of dilemmas

Although the respondents suggested that their social work colleagues were aware of the significance of ARP and ADP in work with BSROs, most of them claimed that this was not optimised with regards to implementation. Indeed, it was suggested that there is a lot of discriminatory practice occurring towards this group that does not fit in with the value systems of ARP or ADP.

Evidence of discrimination in report writing

A common theme that emerged was that when the respondents have 'gatekept' the PSRs of other social workers in their team, they have sometimes noticed that relevant information has often been excluded, or that derogatory references have been incorporated into the reports. The respondents informed me that they fortunately had the opportunity to challenge their colleagues on this issue because of the 'gatekeeping' procedure:

"In the PSR for this young man, my colleague's PSR made no reference to the fact that her client had witnessed and had been subjected to domestic violence by his father, or that he had learning difficulties. Obviously the inclusion of these factors would not serve to condone the young man's offences, but the magistrate must be made aware of the difficulties that he has faced".

"Under the section of the PSR which focuses on providing information about the young person, xxxxx had depicted this young man as being part of a dangerous gang, which wasn't the case. The magistrate would have taken one look at that section and a custodial sentence would've been inevitable".

"I was dismayed that she had stated that he had been excluded from two schools, but had neglected to mention that the Pupil Referral Unit had diagnosed him with dyslexia after he had been referred to them".

These findings support some of the results reported by **Denney (1992)** in his study of racism and anti-racism in the probation service. As was highlighted in chapter two, he discovered that the inclusion of derogatory terms and negative statements were more likely to be evident in the reports of black offenders and this discovery has also surfaced in my study.

It is important to mention that a mixed race social worker emphasised the fact that it is not just white social workers who can use discriminatory language in PSRs. When 'gatekeeping' a PSR, she was appalled by the way in which a Black African colleague had portrayed an Afro-Caribbean BSRO:

"She painted such a grotesque picture of this client's family. She made it seem like the mother, who is Jamaican and a single parent, imposed no boundaries on her children and doesn't care. I know she does, she tries really hard. I've made five home visits to her. Her elder son is my client. I told xxx I didn't agree with the report. There was definitely a cultural issue there".

This finding could allow a powerful argument to be made that there is not only the existence of difficulties relating to BSROs on the basis of race, but also on the basis of understanding their culture. The need for the eradication of cultural racism was recognised by **Dominelli (1997)**, but she based her analysis purely on a white social worker/black client setting, which the aforementioned finding from my study shows is not representative of a broad perspective.

Evidence of discriminatory attitudes in team meetings

Another common theme that emerged was that when cases were discussed in team meetings (whether a social worker is simply feeding back information to the team with regards to the progress on a particular case or whether a case is about to go to court and is brought up for discussion during team meetings), BSROs appear to receive harsher recommendations for sentencing and are spoken about more negatively:

"No other client group gets spoken about with as much negativity as BSROs".

"It's considered good practice not to recommend custody in PSRs for any of our clients when we discuss serious cases in team meetings. Custody has been recommended several times though in the seven months I've been here.....and the clients were all BSROs. In comparison, I've yet to hear a custodial recommendation for a WSRO".

"I've clashed with a few of my team on their heavy and authoritarian suggestions about BSROs.....I tell you".

The social workers generally informed me that they challenged the negativity towards BSROs because they felt that it was unfair.

Direct (negative) feedback from BSROs

Some of the social workers informed me that they have received negative feedback from BSROs themselves, which has suggested to them that this client group has been treated unfairly by some of their social work colleagues. The respondents told me that they made their discoveries when they were on 'duty' (and the social worker of the BSRO was on leave, off sick or at an external meeting):

"When I'm on duty I often see the clients of my colleagues who are away. I sit down with the clients and find out how they are, what they are doing and how helpful we...as an agency are to them. I've had some BSROs give me some pretty negative feedback with regards to how they've been treated, but they won't complain".

"One young man told me that he hates his social worker because he thinks that she is racist. I asked him why he thinks this and he said that she looks down her nose at him and speaks to him rudely. I've heard this before from other……. But I can't go into it".

4.3 Respondents views on their use of the PC, TC and CBT approaches with BSROs

4.3a Positive findings – Disproval of dilemmas

Showing your commitment to ARP and ADP and building the relationship with the client

The social workers reported that it was possible to effectively use the PC, TC and CBT approaches in preventative work with BSROs, but they all related the success of interventions back to the use of ARP (and particularly) ADP. Indeed, the social workers stressed the significance of them being committed to equality and practice that is absence of judgementalism and prejudice. They suggested that this was crucial to developing and maintaining a strong relationship with the client and thus in implementing work that was going to be successful in deterring the BSRO from further offending:

"They have to know that you are sincere and genuine and that you aren't a racist. Once you get them to see these qualities in you, they'll work with you and listen to you".

"Like they say 'the way to a man's heart is through his stomach', I believe that it's the same with BSROs. The way into their hearts and minds is through establishing a rapport. It's only then that you can change their thinking and behaviour. I'm pleased with the way I do that. The use of the models comes naturally and I have a high success rate at deterring my BSROs from reoffending".

"The person-centred approach is so.........important to work with a client group with BSROs. There's no substitute for me showing them that I am a genuine person and demonstrating that I can put myself in their shoes and see the world from their perspective. That's when they open up and trust you. I can then use the TC and CBT models with success".

These findings also suggest that the social workers' use of the PC, TC and CBT approaches are influenced by an approach similar to that developed by **Trotter (1999)**. Indeed, Trotter's pro-social model advocates ways of enabling the client to learn by encouragement. The respondents suggested that encouragement and rapport is essential to successful work with BSROs.

4.3b Negative findings – Confirmation of dilemmas

Reluctance from BSROs

A common theme that emerged from the social workers' responses is in relation to the apparent difficulty that they face in engaging and communicating with BSROs. There was a claim that many BSROs demonstrate reluctance towards their social workers and the interventions that have been selected for them:

"Well X was on an eighteen month Supervision Order and after three months, I was so stressed. I had tried everything to get him to respond fully – talking about myself and my life, how much I despise racism, rap music – and so much more. But it was so....difficult to get him to engage let alone respond to TC or CBT. It was like trying to find water in a desert".

"I've currently got three BSROs and I am having problems with all them. X is on the licence part of his DTO. He was released from X in December. They all seem mistrusting of me and I really do try hard with them. But whatever approach I use.......the result is the same".

The social workers did not attribute the blame to themselves or to the BSROs. There was a consensus amongst the respondents that many BSROs appear to be mistrusting of institutions that they deem to be racist:

"I believe that they feel that YOTs are like other criminal justice agencies – institutionally racist. I think that this makes them hold back".

4.4 Respondents' views on the efficacy of the multi-disciplinary team in their YOT

4.4a Positive findings – Disapproval of dilemmas

Working together towards the same objectives

A common theme that emerged in the social workers' responses is that the multi-disciplinary team is able to work harmoniously to tackle the risk factors that can place BSROs at high risk of re-offending. Indeed, it was suggested by some of the social workers that the expertise and experience of workers from different fields that makes up this "joined up" approach is effective in changing the attitudes and behaviours of a number of BSROs:

"It's great to have workers from other fields working alongside you. It can really make a difference. I mean xxx our education worker helps me get our younger BSROs back into school and those who are aged between 16 to 18 places at college to study a course they actually enjoy. It motivates them to stay clear of re-offending and gives them a chance in life".

"I have had a few BSROs who were committing street robbery to feed their cannabis habit. When they were released from custody and placed on the licence part of their DTO, I have always made an educational and assessment referral to our drugs worker

immediately. One of these clients was determined to stay away from cannabis after seeing xxxx (drugs worker), because he had been made aware of the damage that long-term use could do to his body. He has stayed out of trouble ever since".

4.4b Negative findings – Confirmation of dilemmas

Avoiding conflict with other professionals

A number of the respondents highlighted their frustration that has arisen as a result of the potential conflict that could have occurred between themselves and other members of the multi-disciplinary team. Indeed, this theme was strenuously related to ARP and ADP and the fact that the respondents felt that certain professionals had displayed behaviour and practice towards BSROs that was discriminatory. However, the respondents did not feel comfortable challenging these workers, as although they all work together in the YOT, they are not part of the same team:

"One of my clients who is a BSRO informed me that he was not looking forward to completing his reparation. I thought that this was strange because most clients can't wait to finish their reparation. When I questioned him further, he told me that the police officer who is in charge of this order looked down his nose at him, gave him a lot of dirty looks and spoke to him in a condescending way. He didn't want to complain though. I wanted to challenge this police officer, because it's not the first time a black client has told me this about him, but we are in different teams, we have different managers. It would've created a lot of tension".

"I've wanted to challenge other members for comments I deemed as being racist, but it is hard. Once I ran a group with a colleague and he made a stereotypical comment in front of a group of BSROs. They.......... wouldn't complain. I knew it would cause a lot of ill feeling if I challenged him. Besides when you have different managers it

exacerbates things because my manager would take my side and her manager will take hers. It's a catch 22 situation".

The theme presented here confirms a central finding of the work of **Crawford (1998)**, where he suggested that conflict avoidance is a key drawback of multi-disciplinary teams. He also suggested that this could lead to the neglecting of other significant issues, which with regard to this finding of my study, could be failing to address racist practices.

The respondents suggested that this avoidance can have detrimental effects on groups such as BSROs because when discriminatory attitudes by workers lie unchallenged, such clients lose faith in the system:

"About a dozen BSROs and other black offenders have informed me that they have had derogatory remarks made to them by staff here, but fear of retribution renders them reluctant to complain. They expect me to take action. When I tell them there's little I can do without an official complaint, they have told me that I don't care…but I do".

This again backs up the work of **Crawford (1998)**. Indeed, he argued that multi-disciplinary teams can obscure accountability and further marginalise oppressed groups. The fact that the BSROs mentioned by the respondents were reluctant to complain about the treatment that they received could be argued to be representative of a feeling that nothing would be done (thus representative of a lack of accountability in the YOT).

Lack of ADP training

A common theme that emerged was a widespread belief and assertion that whilst social workers have received vigorous ADP training before they qualified, most of the other members of the multi-disciplinary team have received little or none. The respondents stressed their frustration at the fact that there have been no training days, for the whole team, to make practitioners aware of issues that groups like BSROs face and the practices that should be used and avoided to help them:

"No disrespect, but apart from the social workers, no other members of staff here have had ADP instilled into them".

"I've been working here for three and a half years and we have never been on an ADP course and I think that is disgusting".

It was suggested that this lack of training could result in the alienation of already marginalized groups:

"I mean the young people aren't stupid, but they're vulnerable. If they have workers who can't empathise or understand them, they'll feel....pushed away and victimised. They'll never trust establishments like ours and we'll fail in our objectives".

4.5 Reflecting on ADP issues

Although I will be integrating issues around ADP into my conclusion, which will focus predominately on implications for social work practice with BSROs, I feel that it is important at this stage to briefly reiterate several specific ADP issues from my findings.

Young female BSROs

It was brought to my attention by the respondents that an increasing number of black females are entering the youth justice system. It was suggested by the social workers that these young women generally receive harsher sentences for their offences than their male counterparts. In addition, it was suggested that the same client group may also receive less favourable treatment from workers within the YOT. Taking the predominately negative findings from my research into account, there is a strong possibility that these observations are true.

Learning difficulties and dyslexia

As was discussed earlier in the chapter, a number of social workers highlighted the fact that that some BSROs have learning difficulties and/or dyslexia. Although some of the social workers informed me that they had successfully diagnosed learning difficulties and/or dyslexia in some BSROs, they expressed their concern at the fact that some of their colleagues (past and present) have failed to identify such factors in their assessments. As there is a strong correlation between street robbery and lack of attachment to school **(Fitzgerald et al, 2003)**, improvements in this ADP area are definitely required.

Conclusion

5.0 Conclusion

5.1 Implications for social work practice

Although the findings outlined and discussed in the previous chapter present a positive and negative picture of ARP and ADP social work with BSROs, the majority of the findings unfortunately lean towards the latter.

It was extremely concerning that whilst each of the respondents claimed to be unprejudiced and to be practitioners of the anti-racist and anti-discriminatory approaches, they were technically accusing each other of possessing discriminatory attitudes and practices. This is disturbing in the sense that I had questioned and interviewed the majority of the social workers in theYOT. When I questioned the respondents about their fellow social workers' practice, although almost all of them suggested that their colleagues see ARP and ADP as essential, they suggested that most of them display discriminatory attitudes and practices towards BSROs. It is therefore unlikely that the respondents were referring simply to the social workers who were not interviewed, but that they were actually referring to each other and accusing each other of discriminatory practices. This means that most of the social workers who were claiming to be ARP and/or ADP practitioners actually had these claims contradicted by their colleagues. The implications of this could be detrimental for client groups such as BSROs because a powerful argument could be made that the main objective of the YJB – "to prevent offending by children and young people" **(National Standards, 2002: 3)** – is in jeopardy if social workers are not able to challenge their prejudices and establish strong relationships with their clients. Social workers working with BSROs need to "identify and question their own values and prejudices and their implications for practice", but it would appear that this technique is not widely practised at this YOT.

The findings of my research with regards to other members of the multi-disciplinary team were also predominately negative and this could also have a detrimental impact on the effectiveness of preventative social work with young people such as BSROs. Indeed, if negative occurrences, such as conflict avoidance, continue then barriers may develop between clients and workers (such as that evidenced in pages 45-46) and the success of work in YOTs may falter.

Another concerning implication I must put forward is the fact that Borough X has a poor record of ADP training not only for its social workers, but for **all** of its staff. All of the respondents stressed their frustration at the fact that they have not received training that would help them in their practice with client groups such as BSROs. Indeed, it is becoming more and more recognised that cultural awareness training is crucial to help professionals combat their prejudices, increase their empathy with clients and make more efficacious interventions with them. The mental health campaigning group Mind, for example, has welcomed a recent government report which, amongst other measures, has proposed mandatory cultural awareness training for all mental health professions to tackle institutionalised racism in the field **(The Voice, April 21, 2003)**. If the YJB and its YOTs do not implement a similar strategy, it is likely that the widespread practice of ADP will continue to have a long way to go and groups such as BSROs will continue to be marginalised.

5.2 Concluding remarks and Comments

This Monograph sought to explore ARP and ADP with BSROs in a YOT and I feel that the aims of the study have been met. Indeed the aim of my study was to conduct a study that would signify a movement towards "evidence based" social work practice (see chapter one, p.12) and I feel that the (negative) findings from my research are instrumental in moving towards a "best practice" approach in work with offenders (but particularly with marginalised offenders such as BSROs). Indeed, ARP and ADP, in particular, are such significant areas of social work that they must continually be addressed through evaluation and analysis. A focus on the latter perspective may be more effective though, as this study has demonstrated that it focuses on a number of areas and not just race.

It must be noted that my research may have several limitations though. Firstly, this study was one that was small-scale and limited. Therefore, it may be the case that ADP and/or ARP are practised more effectively in other YOTs. My research is certainly not representative of all YOTs. I would suggest that further research is needed before a definitive claim can be made about the practice of ADP and/or ARP in YOTs. Secondly, I am aware that my study may be biased because of the fact that ARP and ADP are issues that are close to my heart (or that I am 'sensitive' to as discussed on page 20-21) because of my race and culture. I have tried to be as open-minded and objective as possible, but this is not always possible in research. Again, further research may be needed to see if my results are conclusive or not.

References

Abbott, P., et al (1998) ***Research Methods for Nurses and the Caring Professions***. Buckingham: Open University Press.

Audit Commission (1996) ***Misspent Youth: Young People and Crime***. London: Audit Commission.

Bell, J., (1999) ***Doing Your Research Project***. Buckingham: Open University Press.

Borough X (2002) ***Youth Justice Plan***. London: Borough X.

Bryman, A., (1988) ***Quantity and Quality in Social Research***. London: Unwin Hyman.

Cheetham, J., (1982) ***Social Work and Ethnicity***. London: Allen and Unwin.

Cohen, D., (January 30, 2003) "Nearly 15, 000 stabbings, robberies and even murders…most linked to 300 yards where £1m of crack-cocaine is dealt each month. Is this the most dangerous street in Britain? Investigation: The Standard spends 24 hours in the London borough where the police fight their biggest battle against crime", ***Evening Standard*** (p.16).

Coventry Evening Telegraph (September 18, 2002) "Street Crime Worsening, Says Poll" (p.10).

Coventry Evening Telegraph (February 25, 2003) "Man Stabbed in Face in Mugging Horror: Man, 26, Beaten by Gang of Four" (p.1).

Crawford, A., (1998) "Delivering Multi-Agency Partnerships in Community Safety" in Marlow, A., and Pitts, J., (eds.) ***Planning Safer Communities***. Dorset: Russell House Publishing Limited.

Crime and Disorder Act (1998) ***Crime and Disorder Act 1998: Elizabeth II. 1998. Chapter 37***. London: Stationary Office.

Daily Mirror (February 26, 2003) "Blind Woman Mugged for £10" (p.2)

Dean, H., wt al (2000) "Introduction" in Dean, H., et al (eds.) ***Social Policy Review 12***. Newcastle: Social Policy Association

Denney, D., (1992) ***Racism and Anti-Racism in Probation***. London and New York: Routledge.

Dominelli, L., (1997) ***Anti-Racist Social Work – Second Edition***. Basingstoke and London: MacMillian Press Limited.

Fernando, S., Ndegwa, D., and Wilson, M., (1998) ***Forensic Psychiatry, Race and Culture***. London: Routledge.

Fitzgerald, M., (2001) "Ethnic Minorities and Community Safety" in Matthews, R., and Pitts, J., (eds.) ***Crime, Disorder and Community Safety***. London: Routledge.

Fitzgerald, M., et al (2003) ***Young People and Street Crime – Research into Young People's Involvement in Street Crime***. London: Youth Justice Board.

Fuller, R., and Petch, A., (1995) ***Practitioner Research: The Reflective Social Worker***. Buckingham: Open University Press.

Gilroy, P., (1987) ***There Ain't No Black in Union Jack***. London: Hutchinson.

Glaser, B., and Strauss, A., (1967) ***The Discovery of Grounded Theory***. Chicago: Aldine.

Gross, R., (2001) ***Psychology – The Science of Mind and Behaviour – Fourth Edition***. Italy: Hodder and Stroughton Educational.

Hall, S., et al (1978) ***Policing the Crisis-Mugging, the State, and Law and Order***. London and Basingstoke: MacMillian Press Limited.

Haralombos, M., (1995) ***Sociology – Themes and Perspectives: Third Edition***. Collins Educational.

Home Office/Her Majesty's Inspectorate of Constabulary (2000) ***Policing in London: 'Winning Consent' – a Review of Murder Investigation and Community and Race Relations Issues in the Metropolitan Police Service***, London: Home Office.

Home Office (2002) ***Race and the Criminal Justice System: A Home Office Publication under Section 95 of the Criminal Justice Act 1995***. London: Home Office.

Hull, J., (November 21, 1002) "Street Robbery Most Feared Crime in U.K.", ***Independent***, (p.10).

Kinsey, R., et al (1986) ***Losing The Fight Against Crime***. Oxford: Blackwell.

Macpherson, W., (1999) ***The Stephen Lawrence Inquiry: Report of an Inquiry by Sir William Macpherson: Presented to Parliament by the Secretary of State for the Home Department by Command of Majesty, February 1999***. London: Stationary Office.

Mearns, D., and Thorne, B., (1988) ***Person-Centred Counselling in Action***. London: Sage Publications.

Middlesex University (2002) ***Professional Competence and Assessment Planner 2002-2003***. London: Middlesex University.

Milner, J., and O'Byrne, T., (1998) ***Assessment in Social Work***. Basingstoke: MacMillian Press Limited.

Patton, M., (1990) ***Qualitative Evaluation and Research Methods- Second Edition***. London: Publications.

Roberts, B., (1982) "The Debate on 'Sus'" in Cashmore, E., and Troyna, B., (eds.) ***Black Youth in Crisis***. London: George Allen and Unmin.

Rogers, C.R., (1951) ***Client-Centred Therapy***. Boston: Houghton Mifflin Company.

Rubin, A., and Babbie, E., (1997) ***Research Methods for Social Work***. USA: Brooks/Cole Publishing Company.

Scarman, L., (1981) ***The Brixton Disorders 10-12 April – Report on an Inquiry by the R.T. Hon. The Lord Scarman, O.B.E***. London: Her Majesty's Stationary Office.

Scraton, P., and Chadwick, K., (1996) "The Priorities of Critical Criminology" in Muncie, J., et al (eds.) ***Criminological Perspectives – A Reader***. London: Sage Publications.

Sheldon, B., (1992) cited in Denney, D., (1992) ***Racism and Anti-Racism in Probation***. London and New York: Routledge.

Silverman, D., (1993) ***Interpreting Qualitative Data: Methods for Analysing Talk, Text and Interaction***. London: Sage.

Silverman, D., (2000) ***Doing Qualitative Research – A Practical Handbook***. London: Sage Publications.

Sunday Mirror (December 15, 2002) "Woman Stabbed in Street Robbery", (p.16).

Taylor, D., and Veysey, W., (November 7, 2002) "Stop and Search of Black People up by a Third in London", ***Evening Standard*** (p.4).

Teke, Z., (April 21, 2003) "Not Mad, Or Bad, Or Dangerous", **The Voice** (p. 8-9).

Tendler, S., (January 10, 2003) "70% of Muggers are Black in Robbery Hotspots", ***The Times*** (p.11).

The Sun (January 10, 2003) "82% of London Underground Victims Identify Muggers as Being Black" (p.11).

The Sun (April 1, 2003) "Blacks Over-represented in Prison Statistics" (p.7).

Thompson, N., (1997) ***Anti-Discriminatory Practice – Second Edition***. Basingstoke and London: MacMillian Press Limited.

Trotter, C., (1999) ***Working With Involuntary Clients – A Guide to Practice***. London: Sage Publications Limited.

Trower, P., et al (1988) ***Cognitive Behavioural Counselling in Action***. London: Sage.

Quinones, J., (April 7, 2003) "Why Are So Many of our Men in Jail?: New Government Report Reveals Shock Statistics", ***The Voice*** (p.2).

Whittaker, J., (1974) cited in Denney, D., (1992) ***Racism and Anti-Racism in Probation***. London and New York: Routledge.

Williams, C., (1999) "Connecting Anti-Racist and Anti-Oppressive Theory and Practice: Retrenchment or Reappraisal" in ***British Journal of Social Work 29***, 211-230.

Young, J., (1994) ***Policing the Streets – Stops and Search in North London***. London: Islington Council.

Youth Justice Board (November 2002) ***National Standards for Youth Justice***. London: Youth Justice Board.

Appendix

Interview Schedule – Qualitative interviews

- Purpose of research > MA status > Middlesex student
- Thank you for participating in interview
- Confidentiality
- Inform interviewee of their right to refuse to answer any question they feel comfortable about, or to withdraw at any time
- Stress the importance of them anoymising agency and colleagues names in the answering of questions
- Ask whether they object to the interview being taped

1) What do you perceive to be the main issues that black street robbery offenders (BSRO's) face in society (e.g. social exclusion, poverty, racism, lack of education and employment)?

2) What do you perceive to be the main issues that white street robbery offenders (WSRO's) face in society (e.g. social exclusion, poverty, lack of education and employment) ?

3) How do you perceive the treatment of BSRO's in the Criminal Justice System?

4) How do you perceive the treatment of BSRO's in Youth Offending Teams (YOT's)?

5) What do understand by the terms anti-discriminatory practice [1] and anti-racist practice[2]?

6) What are your views on the ways in which YOT social workers use ADP and/or anti-racist practice with BSRO's?

7) What are your views on the ways in which you apply ADP and/or anti-racist practice in your work with BSRO's?

8) How has working in a multi-disciplinary team (with workers like the police, Education workers, Probation Officers and mental health workers) changed/challenged the values of social workers?

---

[1] Where a Social Worker takes account of structural disadvantage and seeks to counter discrimination, on the grounds of race, gender, disability, social class, sexuality and other factors.

[2] Where a Social Worker focuses on the race of the client to gain a deeper understanding of the racism and issues that the client has endured and experienced

9) What are your views on the ways in which other members of the multi-disciplinary team apply ADP and/or Anti-racist practice in their work with BSRO's?

10) How has working in a multi-disciplinary team, with workers like the police, Education workers, Probation Officers and mental health workers) changed/challenged your values?

11) What is your understanding of the person-centred approach[3]?

12) What impact would you say this approach has in work with BSRO's?

13) How do you think its use could be improved in work with BSRO's?

14) What is your understanding of the task-centred approach[4]?

15) What impact would you say this approach has in work with BSRO's?

16) How do you think its use could be improved in work with BSRO's?

17) What is your understanding of cognitive-behavioural therapy[2]?

18) What impact would you say this approach has in work with BSRO's?

19) How do you think its use could be improved in work with BSRO's?

20) What do you see as being the main issues that occur between social workers and BSRO's?

21) What strategies would you like to see devised and implemented to improve the issues that may exist between Social Workers and BSRO's?

- Thank respondent for participating

---

3 Where a Social Worker portrays themselves as being a warm and genuine person in order to gain the trust and respect of the client.

[4] Where the Social Worker and the client agree on tasks, which are central to changing the behaviour and circumstances of the client

[5] Where a Social Worker imparts the client with the knowledge and skills to facilitate the changing of thinking, feeling and behaving